R.E.I. Edition

All our ebooks can be read on the following devices:

- Computer
- eReader
- iOS
- Android
- Blackberry
- Window
- Tablet
- Mobile phone

Mantelli - Brown - Kittel - Graf

Curtiss P-40

ISBN: 9782372975292

Published: January 2025
Also available in Ebook format - ISBN: 9782372971973

www.rei-editions.com

Mantelli - Brown - Kittel - Graf

Curtiss P-40

REI Editions

Index

Curtiss P-40

The Curtiss P-40 was an American-built, single-engine, single-seat monoplane that was used by the Allies as a fighter or fighter-bomber in many theaters of World War II during the first half of the 1940s.

- The Curtiss P-40 Warhawk was the third most produced fighter aircraft by the United States during World War II, after the P-51 and P-47.

Produced by Curtiss Airplane of Buffalo, New York, the P-40 was born from the decision to replace the radial engine of the P-36 Hawk with an inline engine, the first experiment of its kind in the United States. Although the aircraft was very robust and capable as a ground attack aircraft, the result was never an aircraft with exceptional characteristics, due above all to its engine, which was not very powerful at high altitude: it is, therefore, surprising that this aircraft was built in greater numbers than other American fighters during the war, with the exception of the Thunderbolt and the Mustang, and that production continued until the end of 1944.

- This anomaly was even the subject of an investigation by a commission of the American Senate, chaired by Harry Truman, the future president of the United States.

The explanation for this profusion is twofold: at the time it was ordered, American fighter designs favored mixed fighters, capable of fire support in addition to their interception missions. The aircraft was built by Curtiss, which at the time had just invested heavily in increasing its production capacity, which allowed it to deliver large numbers of aircraft in the midst of American and British rearmament.

In 1943, production of the P-40 was supposed to be around 6,000 units: the aircraft that was supposed to replace it on the production lines failed at the prototype stage, leaving enormous capacity available.

- Another 7,000 aircraft were produced, for a total production of 13,738 units.

To improve performance, several avenues were explored: replacing the Allison engine with the Merlin, the Spitfire engine and the one that had transformed the Mustang from a mediocre ground attack aircraft into one of the best fighters of the war.
This route remained blocked for the P-40, because the engines were too valuable to power an aging fighter: in fact, fewer than 2,000 P-40s received Merlin engines.
The second path was the reduction of the aircraft's weight, which allowed the release of the P-40N, the most successful and most built version.
It was one of the tightest-turning monoplane fighters of the war, although at lower speeds it could not outpace highly maneuverable Japanese fighters such as the A6M "Zero" and Ki-43 "Oscar".
The versions supplied to the US armed forces (USAAC and, later, USAAF) were known as:

- Hawk 81, up to the P-40E.
- Warhawk, from the P-40F onwards.

Those delivered to Commonwealth countries, under "lease-lease" arrangements, were known as:

- Tomahawk, equivalent to the P-40A, B and C versions.
- Kittyhawk, equivalent to the P-40D and later versions.

While the P-40 would never truly gain the fame of other aircraft destined to fulfill their roles during World War II, it did, however, manage to carve out a niche for itself in the deserts of Arabia, in the frozen Arctic, and across the Pacific.

- Thus, in the hands of experienced pilots, determined to squeeze the best out of the instruments at hand, the P-40 was more than capable of matching the best the enemy could throw at it.

The P-40's first claim to fame was with the American Volunteer Group (AVG) better known as the Flying Tigers, created to support the Chinese government in repelling the invading Japanese.

Equipped with shark mouths on their front panels, these early aircraft, sometimes operating in desperate conditions, repelled invaders with great skill and held them at bay until America entered the war.

The P-40 also made its mark with the air forces of other countries: in the desert with the RAF and RAAF, across the Pacific with the RAAF and RNZAF and in the frozen north with the RCAF, the Curtiss crossed all skies: the P-40 also saw service with other air forces with Brazil, Turkey and Russia all using it with some success.

In particular, the P-40E combined a robust structure with a firepower that was very respectable for the time: also known among the Commonwealth troops, with the name Kittyhawk Mk I, the P-40E was armed with 6 Browning M2 12.7 mm machine guns installed in the wings. Often characterized by original and visually striking liveries, it was also used as a fighter-bomber thanks to its operational flexibility and the possibility of carrying almost 900 kg of bombs.

History

In the second half of the 1930s, in Europe, both the British and the Germans became convinced of the superiority of inline engines for the propulsion of fighter aircraft, on board which it was important to reduce aerodynamic resistance as much as possible, for example, by eliminating the frontal bulk of a radial engine.

Influenced by the beliefs developed by European aircraft manufacturers, in July 1937 the American armed forces commanders forwarded to the Curtiss Aeroplane and Motor Company a request to develop an inline-engine variant of the Curtiss P-36 Hawk.

The latter, equipped with a Wright star engine, was a relatively modern fighter, having been, together with the Seversky P-35, one of the first all-metal monoplanes equipped with retractable landing gear and a closed cockpit, but by the end of the 1930s it was already giving a glimpse of the need for a more powerful and faster successor.

- An initial test (the XP-37) was carried out with the turbocharged version of the Allison, mounted on a fuselage whose cockpit had been moved back.

On 14 October 1938, the XP-40 prototype, designated Hawk 81 by the manufacturer, made its first flight. It was the result of the installation, on board the tenth production P-36 (number 30-18), of an Allison V-1710-19 engine, a 1,150 hp liquid-cooled V12 engine with a single-stage mechanical supercharger.

Although of equal power, this engine had the advantage of having a smaller frontal section and therefore allowed, through aerodynamic gains, a notable increase in maximum speed.

The front fuselage had been completely redesigned, the carburetor air intake was positioned above the engine cowling and the oil cooler underneath.
The coolant radiator was located under the fuselage, on the leading edge of the wings.
This prototype was followed by thirteen pre-series YP-37s, but the unreliability of the turbochargers quickly slowed the project.

The XP-40 prototype during USAAC testing.

The test and evaluation trials were passed without serious problems, even though the prototype underwent a series of fairly significant modifications in the meantime.
The beginnings were rather disappointing, the aircraft could not exceed 483 km/h and, after some trial and error, an assembly was created under the nose comprising an oil radiator and two for cooling the ethylene glycol mixture.
Additionally , the two lateral exhaust pipes were replaced by six independent ones per side, while the landing gear folding system, inherited from the P-36, was replaced.

- Following these modifications, performance increased and the XP-40 reached 550 km/h, which made it faster than the Hurricane, although inferior to the Spitfire and the Bf 109: however, it had a much greater range than these three aircraft with 976 km, almost double.

In April 1939, the United States Army Air Corps placed an order for 524 examples of the new fighter: among the characteristics of the P-40 that led the USAAC to accept it so enthusiastically were its good speed at low altitude, its rather low price and the prospect of rapid deliveries: both of these last two factors were due to the fact that production of the P-36 was already solidly underway and easily convertible to the new model.

- Furthermore, since the USAAC intended to use the P-40 primarily as a low-altitude tactical support aircraft, the engine's poor power output at high altitude was not a problem.

As the aircraft evolved, and in particular in the transition from an unarmed and unarmored prototype to a fully equipped combat aircraft, its overall weight inevitably increased significantly, further penalising its performance.
The first series of P-40s were armed with two 12.7 mm and two 7.62 mm machine guns as well as six 9 kg (20 lb) bomb launchers under the wings: it had a maximum weight of just over three tons and could reach a speed of 574 km/h.
The definitive version, designated P-40N, had six 12.7 mm machine guns, but could weigh over five tons, with a maximum speed of 552 km/h.
It has a reputation as a fighter aircraft that was outmatched and outclassed by its opponents, which even prompted an investigation after World War II to determine why it had been kept in production against all odds.

In hindsight, it seems, rather, that its pilots had to fight in difficult conditions, which did not allow the aircraft to shine, even if, nevertheless, it had a certain importance in operations in the midst of the Second World War, and this for several reasons:

- The P-39 Airacobra, its most direct competitor, rather disappointed the hopes placed in it.
- The P-47 Thunderbolt became available only in the spring of 1943, and initially in small numbers, shared between several theaters of operation: moreover, it soon showed its limitations as a pure fighter.
- The P-51 Mustang was not available as a fighter until December 1943: it was available in small numbers from the spring of 1943 for reconnaissance missions, in the F-6B/C and A-36 Apache versions.

The P-40 therefore remained, by force of circumstances, until the autumn of 1943, the only valid fighter available in large numbers to the American Air Force, which never used it on the European front.

Although not very efficient at altitude, due to its engine, it served very honourably during much of the conflict, thanks to its low cost, great ease of maintenance and great robustness.

To the British and other Commonwealth nations it was subsequently known as Tomahawk and then Kittyhawk.

The P-40's first claim to fame was with the American Volunteer Group (AVG), better known as the Flying Tigers, created to assist the Chinese government in repelling Japanese invaders. Equipped with shark mouths on their nose panels, these early aircraft, sometimes operating in desperate conditions, repelled the invaders with great skill and held them off until America entered the war: it remains, therefore, famous as the aircraft of the Flying Tigers of the 14th USAAF engaged in China during

World War II, and has also been the aircraft of numerous aces from various countries.
The last examples to serve in an air force were Brazilian: they were not retired until 1958.
The P-40 was, therefore, for two years the most widespread fighter in the American air force: in fact, immediately after Pearl Harbour, the American authorities were looking for a good performing aircraft that could be mass-produced in a short time and the only aeronautical industry ready in that period was Curtiss with the P-40.

Technique

The Curtiss P-40 was a low-wing monoplane with an all-metal structure, featuring an overall conventional architecture, typical of most single-engine, single-seat fighters of World War II.
The two half-wings that made up the wing were joined at the axis of the airplane, and their backs constituted the floor of the cockpit: the wing structure was very robust, being based on five spars, beams arranged parallel to the opening, reinforced and connected to each other by light alloy slabs, ribs and stringers.

- The cladding sheets were attached to the structure by rivets with a drowned head.

The wings had a substantially trapezoidal plan shape, with rounded wingtips: the leading edge had a slight backward sweep, while the trailing edge was occupied along its entire length by the flaps and the fabric-covered ailerons, which ensured roll control.
The landing gear was of the rear tricycle type, and was completely retractable: the two front legs, which made up the main landing gear, disappeared inside fairings in the belly of the wing thanks to a rearward rotation and a further 90° rotation of the wheels around the axis of the legs themselves: the rear wheel retracted backwards into the fuselage, and its housing was closed by two small doors.
The fuselage was connected to the wing by large aerodynamic fittings, and housed a relatively spacious cockpit equipped with an armoured windscreen and a rearward-sliding canopy.
The pilot was protected, front and rear, by armour for a total of 80 kg, and had a machine gun and a reflex collimator.

- The fuselage structure consisted of sixteen transverse frames and several longitudinal stringers.

The empennage was attached to the rear part of the fuselage, characterised by a straight leading edge, with a marked sweep angle, and curved trailing edges.
The structure, both of the fixed surfaces, stabilizer and fin, and of the mobile ones, elevator and rudder, was completely metallic: the fixed surfaces had four spars each and were covered, like all the rest of the aircraft, with metal sheets.
The movable ones had only one spar and were equipped with a fabric covering: on the other hand, all the control surfaces, including the ailerons, were equipped with aerodynamic compensations, correction flaps and counterweights.

- The powertrain, installed at the front and separated from the passenger compartment by a firewall, was supported by an engine mount made of welded metal tubes.

The cowling that protected the engine was made up of panels and sheets that could be opened and removed to ensure the easiest possible access to the engine and radiators.
The two radiators responsible for cooling the ethylene glycol for engine cooling were housed, together with the smaller oil radiator for cylinder lubrication, in a large structure under the propeller hub.
The shape of the large radiator fairing suggested to many operational units showy decorations; the most famous of these is the "shark mouth" one of Claire Chennault's Flying Tigers.
The P-40's engine was the Allison V-1710, a twelve-cylinder 60° V engine that, when it entered service in the late 1930s, had aroused great expectations, which, however, were soon to be disappointed.

- The performance of the V-1710, in fact, always left much to be desired, especially at high altitude, and in all the aircraft on which it was mounted it gave unsatisfactory results.

The engine's nominal power output varied throughout the aircraft's evolution, from the 1,054 hp of the V-1710-33 mounted on the P-40B to the 1,373 hp of the V-1710-73 mounted on the P-40K: however, as the aircraft lacked a turbocharger system, available power dropped significantly as altitude increased.
To overcome this problem, another engine was installed on some versions (P-40F and P-40L), the Packard V-1650, the American version, produced under license, of the Rolls Royce Merlin, but its limited availability prevented its widespread use on the P-40.

- The P-40 was, however, equipped with a centrifugal supercharger supercharging system.

The propeller, faired with a large spinner, was a three-bladed Curtiss, whose blades were hollow, made of steel, and thanks to a reduction gear it rotated more slowly than the crankshaft.
The propeller pitch was variable by hand or automatically to maintain a constant rpm.
The 100 octane petrol that powered the engine was contained in three tanks, for a total of 558 litres:

- One, of 236 litres, located behind the passenger compartment.
- Two, of 132 and 190 litres, arranged, one behind the other, in the central section of the wing, under the cockpit.

To these could be added additional drop tanks, carried under the fuselage, for a further 197 litres.
The P-40's fixed armament varied considerably over the course of the aircraft's evolution:

- Early versions had two 7.62 mm machine guns installed in the thickness of the wing and two 12.5 mm mounted above the engine, synchronized to fire through the propeller disc.

- The P-40E and later versions, on the other hand, were equipped with six 12.7 mm guns installed in two groups of three in the two wing halves: equipped with 281 rounds each, they guaranteed a total of 11 or 12 seconds of fire.

The maximum bomb load was normally 317 kg, although in exceptional cases the aircraft could take off, overloaded, with two 227 kg bombs, for a total war load of 454 kg.
The P-40 was equipped with a hydraulic system, responsible for the extension and retraction of the landing gear and the extension of the flaps, an electrical system, which powered the radio, and systems for supplying oxygen to the pilot and for heating the cockpit.

The P-40 was a truly inexpensive aircraft, if we refer to the average costs of various USAAF fighters (unit prices in 1944):

- Lockheed P-38 Lightning: $97,147
- Republic P-47 Thunderbolt: $85,578
- Republic P-43 Lancer: $85,694
- Bell P-39 Airacobra: $50,666
- North American P-51 Mustang: $51,572
- Curtiss P-40: $44,892

Costs of different P-40 models:

- P-40: $51,538, including airframe 24,889, engine 17,126, propeller 3,425, electronics 1,360.

- P-40E: $59,618, including airframe 27,482, engine 16,885, propeller 2,481, electronics 3,160.
- P-40N: $52,869, including airframe 27,189, engine 10,702, propeller 3,110, electronics 7,154.

Technical features

Dimensions and weights

- Length: 10.16 meters
- Wingspan: 11.38 meters
- Height: 3.23 meters
- Wing area: 21.93 m^2
- Empty weight: 2,812 Kg
- Maximum take-off weight: 5,170 kg

Propulsion

- Engine: Allison V-1710-81
- Power: 1,377 hp (1,014 kW)

Performance

- Maximum speed: 563
- Range: 545 km – 2,253 km with additional tanks
- Tangency: 9,450 meters

Armament

- Machine guns: 6 x 12.7 mm Browning M2
- Bombs: 1 x 227 kg

Unit cost

- $25,000 (first series)

Specimens

- 13,738, considering all versions

Allison V-1710 Engine

The Allison V-1710 was a 60° V12 aircraft engine manufactured by the American Allison Engine Company and used on USAAF aircraft during World War II.

- The V-1710 was the only engine of this type designed and produced in the USA during this conflict to be used in combat: its debut was not the best due to some inconveniences related to the supercharging system but later, thanks to subsequent developments, it became a powerful and reliable engine.

The Allison Engine Company, a part of General Motors, began designing a liquid-cooled engine in 1929 in response to a request from the U.S. Army for a 1,000 hp (750 kW) engine for use in new bombers and fighters.
To facilitate production and installation, the engine had to be equipped with various reduction gears and a turbocharger.
In this way, engines could be produced from the same production line that could be mounted on any aircraft.
The Great Depression slowed development and it was not until 14 December 1936 that the engine was flown for the first time fitted to a Consolitated XA-11A.
On 23 April 1937, the V-1710-C6 passed the 150-hour test required by the US Army.

- Power output, 1,000 hp, was in line with demand and the Allison engine was one of the first production aircraft engines to achieve it.

Once the tests were passed, the engine was offered to all aircraft manufacturers: the new American fighters, which were being designed at that time, were all built around this unit.

- The engine was then used on the Lockheed P-38, the Curtiss P-40 and the Bell P-39 Airacobra: North American also chose it for its P-51A Mustang.

Initially it was decided to focus only on low altitude performance, as it was believed that the problem of high altitude operation would be solved with further developments in turbocharging, thus outperforming the engines then produced in Europe which, instead, were equipped with mechanical compressors.
With the outbreak of the conflict, however, there was a high demand for heat-resistant alloys, particularly tungsten, which led to a limitation in the production of turbines.
The USAAF decided to concentrate the availability of these components on bomber engines, which at the time had a higher priority.
For the V-1710 the result was the adoption of an underdeveloped, single-stage mechanical compressor that proved satisfactory only at low altitudes: only in the final versions was a two-stage compressor introduced that significantly improved the engine's performance.
These versions were chosen for mounting on the Bell P-63 Kingcobra, the North American P-82 Twin Mustang and several experimental aircraft.
The last operational use of the engine occurred on the 250 P-82s built immediately after the end of the conflict and used until the early 1950s.

- At the end, production stood at 70,000 units.

All will be built at the Allison plant in Indianapolis, Indiana.
In addition to aviation, the V-1710 also found other uses.
Immediately after the war, the availability of a large number of surplus engines made this engine accessible to those who

wanted to use it in drag racing or in general in all competitions requiring high power.

- In some cases, power was increased to 4,000 hp (3,000 kW), a value not even imagined at the time of its design.

Still in the aeronautical field, the engine found new life with the emergence of the so-called Warbird movement, aircraft from the Second World War restored and brought back to flying conditions, which widely used the V-1710 both on the airframes that mounted it at the time, and as a replacement on those aircraft whose engines have now disappeared.
The V-1710 benefited from General Motors' construction philosophy and versatility in installing different components.
The engine could be considered to consist of two parts.

- The central part consisted of the engine itself: on this standard central core, various accessories could then be mounted, in the rear part, and reduction groups, in the front part, thus satisfying the different needs of all aircraft.

Furthermore, this approach made it very simple to replace both the supercharging system and to change the compression ratio , allowing for a range of engines that could be effective from 2,400 metres up to 7,900 metres.
In the engines used by the P-63 and P-39, the V-1710-E, the front reduction gear was moved forward and connected to the engine, located in the central part of the aircraft, with a long transmission shaft, while in the V-1710-F engines, mounted on the other aircraft, the P-40, P-38, P-51A and P-82, the gear was integral with the engine.

- Another feature of the V-1710 was the ability to rotate the propeller both clockwise and counterclockwise quite easily.

During construction, in fact, a special crankshaft was assembled, a series of gears for the supercharging system, a series of accessories and a starting system that was appropriate for the chosen direction of rotation.

- The V-1710 was often criticized for the lack of a mechanical supercharger for high altitudes.

Usually, this criticism is made by comparing the later versions of the Merlin produced under license in the United States such as the Packard V-1650, equipped with a two-stage supercharger. The engine, however, was designed, following the requests of the US Army, with only a single-stage turbocharger and if better performance at higher altitudes had been required, a new type of turbine could have been mounted.

The first V-1710s had a maximum combat altitude limited to 5,000 metres, but being available in large numbers they were widely used especially in the North African theatre of operations.

Allison later also developed a V-1710 with a two-stage supercharger which was fitted to the P-63 and P-82.

- By the end of the conflict, 60% of fighters produced in the United States were equipped with the V-1710.

The company constantly developed and improved its engine so that if at the beginning it supplied 1,000 hp (750 kW) in the final versions, V-1710-143/-145 (G6R/L), thanks also to the developments obtained in fuels it reached 2,200 hp (1,600 kW).

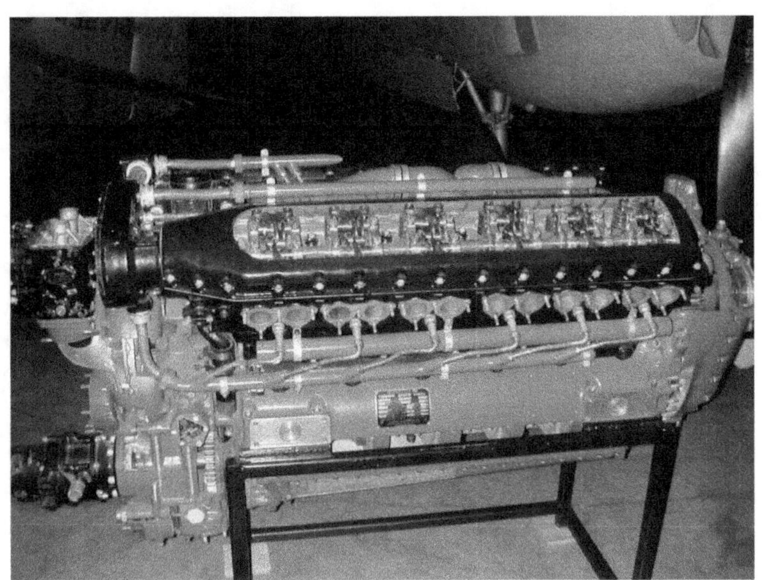

A sectioned Allison V-1710.

Allison then approved an emergency combat power level that allowed an engine providing 1,150 hp (860 kW) at takeoff to be boosted to 1,600 hp (1,200 kW): however, if this power was used, the engine had to be completely disassembled and overhauled before being used again.

- The production cost of the engine, thanks to improvements in its industrialization, also steadily decreased during the conflict: at the beginning, a V-1710 cost 25,000 dollars while later the cost per unit dropped to 8,500 US dollars.

The engine's useful life increased from the initial 300 hours to 1,000 in the less powerful versions: these developments were achieved with a minimal increase in total weight.

Technical Features Allison V-1710

- Number of cylinders: 12 in 60° V
- Cooling: Pressurized liquid, 70% water and 30% ethylene glycol
- Power supply: Bendix Stromberg carburetor with automatic fuel regulator
- Distribution: SOHC 4 valves per cylinder. Exhaust valves with sodium insert
- Compressor: Single stage centrifugal
- Length: 2,502 mm
- Width: 744 mm
- Height: 1,046 mm
- Displacement: 28.03 L
- Bore: 139.7 mm
- Stroke: 152.4mm
- Compression ratio: 6.65:1
- Empty weight: 655 kg
- Power: 1,325 hp (988 kW) at 3,000 rpm
- Power-to-weight ratio: 1.51 kW/kg
- Fuel: 100 octane gasoline

Versions

The P-40 was one of the Allied aircraft of World War II produced in the greatest number of versions.
There were so many of them that in some cases they confused even the Allied pilots.

XP-37

By 1937 the USAAC realized that the Hawk 75 was inferior to European aircraft and so requested that a P-36 be converted to an Allison V-1710 inline engine.
The prototype had the 1710-11 version of the turbocharged engine, producing 1,150 hp and was designated XP-37. The cockpit was moved back towards the tail to make room for the turbocharger, the engine was liquid-cooled with two radiators on either side of the nose.
Armament was one 7.62 mm Browning M1919 machine gun and one 12.7 mm Browning M2 machine gun, both in the nose.
The XP-37 continually had problems with the turbocharger and with the pilot's visibility.

YP-37

In 1938 another batch of 13 prototypes derived from the Model 75I was ordered with a V-1710-21 engine and a more reliable supercharger in a newly designed nose.
The project was cancelled as visibility problems persisted and the turbocharger continued to give problems.

XP-40

Military serial number 38-010: prototype characterised by the radiator located behind the wing.
A 1,150 hp Allison V-1710-19 engine without a turbocharger was fitted, so the cockpit was again moved forward, improving visibility, and the radiator was moved to a ventral position, under the nose, while various other modifications were made to the aircraft during testing: among other things, the design of the engine exhausts and the structure of the landing gear were changed.
Armament consisted of two 12.7mm Browning M2 cannons mounted in the nose.

P-40

Known as the P-40A for export, designated Tomahawk Mk I by the British: 140 of which were requested by France, it was used by the RAF for training and ground attack purposes.
Another 200 examples were delivered to the USAAC.
Allison V-1710-33 engine, 1,040 hp.
It was armed with two 12.7 mm machine guns in the fuselage and two 7.7 mm machine guns in the wing.
This version was not considered ready for combat, as it was still lacking in armament and armour, but due to the shortage of fighters the RAF employed them anyway, in North Africa.

P-40B

Tomahawk Mk II: Heavy armour version with pilot protection and self-sealing fuel tanks.
131 were delivered to the USAAC and 110 to the RAF.
As mentioned, the initial examples had shown some shortcomings, in particular poor passive protection, so, in the P-

40B, the armour behind the cockpit was increased and 4 7.62 mm MG machine guns were added to each wing.

Dimensions and weights

- Length: 9.66 meters
- Wingspan: 11.38 meters
- Height: 3.76 meters
- Wing area: 21.92 m2
- Empty weight: 2,535 Kg
- Maximum take-off weight: 3,447 kg

Propulsion

- Engine: 1 Allison V-1710-33
- Power: 1,040 hp

Performance

- Maximum speed: 566 km/h
- Climb speed: 14.65 m/sec
- Autonomy: 1,173 km
- Tangency: 9,875 meters

Armament

- Machine guns: 2 x 12.7 mm plus 4 x 7.62 mm

P-40C

Further improvement with better armored tanks.
Due to the ever-increasing overall weight, the performance of these early series, all powered by the 1,054 hp Allison V-1710-33, gradually deteriorated.
They had 507-litre (134-gallon) self-sealing tanks with provision for an additional 197-litre (52-gallon) tank.
Weights: 2,636-3,400-3,655 kg.

Speed dropped to only 554 km/h at 4,570 metres, still almost at the level of a Bf-109E, especially considering the altitude, with a range of around 1,173-1,550 km, a ceiling of around 9,000 metres and a climb of around 770 metres/min.
They quickly saw service overseas, notably with the 15th and 18th Groups in Hawaii, and then with the 20th in the Philippines.
During the attack on Pearl Harbor on December 7, over sixty aircraft were destroyed on the ground: a few took off but without success, even though they claimed a total of 5 victories. By the end of the day, only 25 serviceable aircraft remained.
Something similar happened in the Philippines, with a simultaneous attack by the Japanese.
The export type was the Tomahawk IIB of which as many as 930 were built, mostly for the USSR, RAF and SAAF.

P-40D

Kittyhawk Mk I: Extensively redesigned model, with shortened fuselage and enlarged radiator, fitted with a new 1,166 hp Allison V-1710-39 engine, capable, in emergencies, of producing up to 1,470 hp for 5 minutes.
The empty weight increased to 2,816 kg and the fully loaded weight to a whopping 3,996 kg.
The nose guns disappeared, and were moved to the wings, bringing the total armament to four 12.7 mm machine guns, all wing-mounted with provision for two 20 mm cannon, one in each wing.
It first flew in May 1941, and 582 were produced, of which 560 entered RAF service.

P-40E

Kittyhawk Mk IA: Weighted version with armament increased to six 12.7 mm machine guns in the wings.
It was slightly heavier than its predecessor and had a speed of 570 km/h.

Curtiss P-40E Warhawk displayed at the National Museum of the United States Air Force in Dayton, Ohio (USA).

Its rate of climb was just 640 meters/min, and it took 11.5 minutes to reach 6,096 meters, with a ceiling of 8,800 meters.
First variant produced in large series, 2,320 units were built.

Dimensions and weights

- Length: 9.66 meters
- Wingspan: 11.38 meters
- Height: 3.76 meters
- Wing area: 21.92 m^2
- Empty weight: 2,880 kg

- Maximum take-off weight: 4,000 kg

Propulsion

- Engine: 1 Allison V-1710-39
- Power: 1,150 hp

Performance

- Maximum speed: 585 km/h
- Climbing speed: 10.70 m/sec
- Autonomy: 1,050 km
- Tangency: 8,840 meters

Armament

- Machine guns: 6 x 12.7 mm with 281 rounds each
- Bombs: 680 kg

P-40F

Kittyhawk Mk II: Resulting from the installation on a P-40D airframe of a new engine, the 1,318 hp Packard V-1650-1, the Rolls-Royce Merlin produced under license in the USA, it was the first Warhawk equipped with a truly adequate engine.

The idea came from some English engineers who had noticed that the Mustangs and P-40s with Allison engines lost power at altitude while their Hurricanes and Spitfires, with their Merlin engines, did not have this problem.

Featuring significantly better performance than previous types, only 1,311 were built due to the limited availability of the Merlin engine.

All but the first 250 P-40Fs featured a fuselage approximately 50 cm longer than previous versions and were also recognisable by the absence of the carburetor air intake above the nose.

Over 1,300 built, all with the stretched fuselage of the P-40F.

Dimensions and weights

- Length: 11.38 meters
- Wingspan: 11.38 meters
- Height: 3.76 meters
- Wing area: 21.92 m^2
- Empty weight: 2,990 kg
- Maximum take-off weight: 4,238 kg

Propulsion

- Engine: Packard V-1650-1
- Power: 1,300 hp

Performance

- Maximum speed: 585 km/h
- Rate of climb: 3,048 meters in 4.5 min, 6,100 meters in 11.6 min
- Autonomy: 1,125 km
- Tangency: 10,500 meters

Armament

- Machine Guns:
  - 4 or 6 M2 12.7mm with 240-312 rounds each
- Bombs: 2 x 227 kg

P-40G

Minor version, only 45 produced, with lightened armament, six 7.7 mm machine guns, and wings built to RAF specifications.

YP-40F and XP-40K

Experimental versions aimed at improving the aerodynamic refinement of the project.

P-40K

Kittyhawk MK III: Return to the Allison engine in the improved 1,373 hp V-1710-73 version.
The K series was intended to be the last of the P-40s as work was underway on the development of its successor, the P-60.
An order was placed for 600 P-40Ks, all destined for China; however, development of the P-60 was cancelled and the United States entered the war, so the order was increased to 1,300 P-40Ks, which were similar aircraft to the P-40E, with minor modifications including a different ammunition stowage system that remedied the jamming problems that had arisen. This version was the heaviest of the P-40s and at low altitudes the aircraft proved to have good characteristics.
As had happened with the P-40F, also in this case the increase in engine power created stability problems and therefore the size of the fin was increased in the first production examples while subsequently the larger tail was adopted as in the P-40F5.

This modification was retained in all subsequent versions of the aircraft.

Dimensions and weights

- Length: 11.38 meters
- Wingspan: 11.38 meters
- Height: 3.76 meters
- Wing area: 21.92 m^2
- Empty weight: 2,990 kg
- Maximum take-off weight: 4,240 kg

Propulsion

- Engine: Allison V-1710-73
- Power: 1,373 hp

Performance

- Maximum speed: 582 km/h
- Rate of climb: 11.5 minutes to 6,096 meters
- Autonomy: 1,100 km
- Tangency: 10,485 meters

Armament

- Machine guns: 4 x 12.7 mm M2
- Bombs: 2 x 227 kw

P-40J

The P 40 J was to be equipped with a turbocharged engine to obtain better performance at altitude, but the development of the P-40F model with Merlin engine led to the abandonment of that model.

In May 1942 all development of the J version was cancelled before series production began.

P-40L

The version was derived from the P-40F, had a Merlin engine but was lightened, reducing the armour protecting the cockpit and the ammunition of the machine guns.
The overall weight was therefore greatly reduced by lightening the armament, brought to four 12.7 mm machine guns, eliminating part of the armour and limiting the fuel load.
For these reasons the version was jokingly nicknamed by the crews "Gypsy Rose Lee", after a famous American stripper.
700 of these were built.

P-40M

Kittyhawk Mk III: version completely similar to the P-40K, from which it differed only in its engine, a 1,217 hp Allison V-1710-81.

P-40M Kittyhawk.

Nearly all 600 of the aircraft produced, as well as a good portion of the P-40Ks, were delivered to the RAF and were also used by Commonwealth air forces.
Although this model had a less powerful engine, it was lighter and the climbing speed improved considerably.

P-40N

The last important model was the one produced in the greatest number of units: 5,219.

- It initially resulted from the union of the 1,217 hp V-1710-81 with a lightened P-40L/M airframe and equipped with a new type of windshield.

In an effort to improve performance, Curtiss worked on weight reduction by lightening the aircraft with a new airframe design, smaller landing gear wheels, the removal of two machine guns, and the introduction of aluminum oil and coolant radiators.
The N-1 to N-10 series, armed with only four 12.7 mm machine guns, were among the lightest and fastest produced, but later, particularly with the N-15 to N-40 series, weight increased again and performance dropped despite the adoption of the 1,373 hp V-1710-73.
Starting with the P-40N-5 series, a new canopy was introduced which improved the pilot's visibility and the machine guns returned to six under the wings and could also be attached to bombs or droppable fuel tanks.
Of the 5,219 examples produced since 1943:

- Britain received 586, under the designation Kittyhawk IV, but the first 130 were sold to the Soviet Union.
- Australia received 468.
- New Zealand 172.
- Canada 36.

- Brazil 41.

The P-40N-5-CU "Little Jeanne". This aircraft was flown by USAAF Lieutenant Robert Warren of the 7th Fighter Squadron, 49th Fighter Group, during World War II. The aircraft was abandoned at Tadji, Papua New Guinea, then recovered in 1974 and restored to flying condition in Australia in 2002.

P-40P

Version designed to be powered by Merlin engines: however, due to the shortage of the British engine, the project was cancelled and the aircraft ordered were delivered as P-40N

XP-40Q

Experimental version, after 1943, designed with the idea of postponing the inexorable aging process that was making the P-40 obsolete.

It was characterized by its lightened structure, armament consisting of four 12.7 mm machine guns, a 1,442 hp Allison V-

1710-121 engine, a four-bladed propeller and a teardrop canopy that guaranteed the pilot excellent visibility in flight.
During testing it reached 679 km/h, but did not pass the experimental stage.

Flying the P-40

The P-40 was an initially capable aircraft.
Among the very first to enter into action at Pearl Harbor, together with the P-36s, it achieved several victories as early as December 7, 1941.
However, against Axis fighters it was surpassed, although much also depended on tactics: among the USAAF units, generally equipped with the high-performance, albeit rather heavy, P-40F or L, the "Chickentail" group should be mentioned, which had a good kill-loss ratio.
Overall, however, the P-40s, especially those of the SAAF, became destined victims for hunters like Marseille and fighter groups like JG27.

- The Macchi 202s themselves, although lightly armed, were a more than worthy enemy.

And there were many: in June 1942, intelligence had a quantity of information which among other things included, under the 5th Air Squadron, something like 104 C.202s: 47, of which 40 ready (71 day pilots) for the First Wing; another 57 for the Fourth (47 ready) with 58 pilots.
This meant 104 aircraft in total, of which 87 were currently serviceable, the other 17 were still under repair and would be repaired sooner or later.
Another 63 MC.200s of which 52 ready with 64 day pilots and 12 night pilots were in the 2nd Wing, and, finally, there were 32 bombers (of which 19 ready) Z.1007, and various units with the CR.42, S-79 and G.50.
In short, 167 fighters that were either slightly inferior to the P-40s, or significantly superior.

- Even considering the serviceable aircraft, there were still 139 aircraft ready, the equivalent of about 8 squadrons of 18 aircraft each.

And this obviously did not include the Bf-109Fs: had they been more or less like the Macchi MC.202s, they would have been 200 first-choice fighters against nothing or almost nothing (there were the introduction early Spitfire Mk V Trop), and what's more they were aircraft used almost exclusively for free-hunting missions, rather than loaded with bombs and sent out to strafe targets on the ground.
But then again, this is how the DAF stopped the Axis advance and later, despite losses, won the war in Africa: the Axis fighters, too busy fighting their counterparts, managed to do very little against the bombers.

- The P-40, at low altitude, could outmaneuver the Bf-109, outfire, and outlast it; the only way the Bf-109 could win was to fight “vertically” with fast dives and climbs.

Note that the Allison had a fuel injection system, which allowed it, unlike the Merlin, to nosedive without losing power during acceleration.
The new P-40N could have been a remarkable answer to the demand for high performance: despite its rather limited power, at about 3,000 meters it could exceed 600 km/h: that is, it could go faster than even a Bf-109G.
But it didn't last long: soon the machine guns returned to six, and the aircraft was weighed down by tanks, bombs of up to 680 kg and so on, so much so that it was effectively used only as a fighter-bomber.
The speed then dropped to about 550 km/h, even worse than the other P-40s, but on the other hand it is admirable that, with a power no greater than that of an MC.202, this heavy aircraft

could still fly faster, especially at low altitude, where it normally operated, and indeed, decidedly very fast.
As for the Allison-engined Kittyhawk I, it had a climb of 8.5 m/sec at 3,500 meters and a ceiling of 8,840 meters, but with the Merlin it could climb at 8.1 m/sec at 5,200 meters, a ceiling of 10,450 meters, and greater speed.
With the Allison there was no automatic control of the carburetor pressure, so it was necessary to be very careful on take-off, especially with the throttle which could go beyond the stop.
After takeoff, a button had to be held down for more than half a minute to retract the landing gear.

- The maximum speed was found by the British to be less good than declared: 530 km/h at 4,570 metres.

The improved Merlin types, among other things, were equipped with separate emergency hydraulic systems, the trim was electric with a lateral control, and was useful for dives, to assist the ailerons in a dive, when they inevitably became heavy.
The ailerons were light and very effective in handling the P-40, while the rudder was, however, rather hard to operate, and sometimes jammed if pushed beyond a certain angle.

Use

The first P-40s were expected to enter service with the Armée de l'air, the French air force, during 1940.
However, when France surrendered to the invading German forces on 25 June of that year, none of the 140 aircraft ordered by the French had yet been delivered, and so in July the entire order was taken over by the British Royal Air Force.
The United Kingdom placed orders for another 1,000 aircraft, and named the aircraft it received Tomahawk Mark I: the United States had to delay the entry into service of its P-40s to give priority to the British, and the first 200 USAAC examples did not reach operational units until 1941.
The British, however, soon discovered the limitations of the P-40, especially in high-altitude combat, and so they assigned the model to the North African theatre of operations, while in the European theatre, where the prospect of a German invasion of Great Britain seemed to be getting ever closer, they retained the Hawker Hurricane and Supermarine Spitfire units for the defence of the mother country.

- In North Africa the RAF Tomahawk Mk Is were soon joined by the Tomahawk Mk IIs, with improved armament and armour: both gave satisfactory results as fighter-bombers, a role in which they were advantaged by good robustness and a considerable warload, as well as good low-altitude performance.

France did, however, end up employing some P-40Ls, which fought in Tunisia in 1943 under the banner of the GC II/3 Lafayette fighter group, part of the Forces aériennes françaises libres, the air force of Free France, which in turn depended on the Gaullist armed forces.

- Shortly after the US entered the war following the Japanese attack on Pearl Harbor, around one hundred Tomahawk Mk IIAs were taken from a contract intended for the RAF and sent to Nationalist China, where they equipped the 1st American Volunteer Group, better known by the nickname of the Flying Tigers, under the command of General Claire Chennault.

Initially part of the Nationalist Chinese Air Force, the Chung-Hua Min-Kuo K'ung-Chün, the Flying Tiger volunteers later regularly joined the United States Army Air Force, where they came under the authority of the XVI Air Force.

In the early period of the war, between December 1941 and July 1942, when the 1st AVG transformed into the USAAF's 23rd Fighter Group, the Flying Tigers successfully held off the better-equipped and more numerous Japanese forces.

- Although the P-40 was substantially inferior to Japanese aircraft, particularly the Mitsubishi A6M, the Flying Tigers managed to destroy 286 enemy aircraft while losing only 23 men, although post-war cross-checks suggest that the number of opponents shot down may have been appreciably lower than reported.

In large part, this success was due to the innovative approach to air combat preached by Chennault, who had carefully studied Japanese tactics and equipment, as well as the tactics of Soviet pilots in China and the strengths and weaknesses of his own men and aircraft.

The Flying Tigers never numbered more than 62 airworthy crews, and Chennault was further challenged by the fact that many of his volunteers had no real combat experience: however, he was able to turn these problems to his advantage, relegating unfit pilots to secondary duties and ensuring that he always had substantial reserves.

- His combat tactics involved attacking enemies in groups from a higher altitude, diving into them and then quickly disengaging, avoiding at all costs engaging in close-range maneuvered combat, since the P-40s were neither as maneuverable nor as numerous as the Japanese aircraft.

In addition, the Flying Tigers had the important tactical support of a vast observation and warning network spread across China, composed of people, telephones, radios and telegraph lines that provided information on enemy attacks and directed interceptors towards them, guided aid to crashed pilots and indicated to intelligence experts the location of the wreckage of downed enemy aircraft.

- The Curtiss P-40, which the Soviets, like the British, referred to as the Tomahawk or Kittyhawk, was the first Allied aircraft supplied to the Soviet Union under the Lend-Lease agreement.

In total, the Soviet Air Force and Naval Aviation operated 2,097 P-40s.

146 Tomahawks were shipped to the Soviet Union from Britain and another 49 arrived from the United States: many aircraft arrived incomplete, missing their wing machine guns and even the lower part of the engine cowling.

By the end of September 1941, however, the first 48 examples had been assembled and began testing.

Test flights revealed several flaws: the generator and oil pump gears frequently failed, forcing Soviet pilots to make frequent crash landings.

- The final report on the tests conducted stated that the Tomahawk was inferior to Soviet aircraft equipped with the M-105P engines with regard to horizontal speed and rate of climb.

However, the aircraft showed good characteristics in terms of the ability to operate from short runways, horizontal handling, range and robustness.

- Although they were not entirely convinced by the P-40, the Soviets soon put it on the front lines.

The first unit to receive the American aircraft was the 126th IAP, which was deployed on the Soviet Western Front and the Kalinin Front.
The unit went into action on 12 October 1941, and by 15 November 1941 had already claimed 17 Luftwaffe aircraft shot down.
However, Lieutenant Smirnov claimed that the P-40's armament was rather ineffective in air combat, although it was sufficient for strafing enemy lines.

- Similarly, another Soviet pilot, SG Ridnyy (Hero of the Soviet Union), emphasized that to shoot down an enemy aircraft he had to fire half of his shots from a distance of 50–100 meters.

In January 1942, approximately 198 sorties were flown, for a total of 334 flight hours, and 11 combats with German aircraft took place, during which 5 Messerschmitt Bf 109s, a Junkers Ju 88 and a Heinkel He 111 were shot down.

What emerges from these data is the fact that , as also confirmed by the pilots' reports on the circumstances of the combat, the P-40 was able to hold its own with some success against the Bf 109, one of the best fighters available to Germany in the first part of the war.
For example, on 18 January 1942 Lieutenants S.V. Levin and IP Levsha engaged a formation of seven Bf 109s in tandem, managing to shoot down two of them without suffering any losses.

A few days later, on 22 January, three more P-40s, under the command of Lieutenant E.E. Lozov, engaged 13 enemy Bf 109Es, shooting down two, again without losses.

- In total, in January, only two P-40 Tomahawks were lost, one to German flak, and another shot down by a Messerschmitt.

The Soviet Union's P-40s saw most of their front-line use between 1942 and early 1943: the model was used on the northern sectors of the front and played an important role in the defense of Leningrad.
The most represented types were the P-40B, C, E, K and M.

- By the time the improved P-40F and N versions became available, production of Soviet aircraft of satisfactory performance had grown sufficiently to allow the Curtiss fighters to be replaced by the new Lavochkin La-5 and several types of Yakovlev fighters.

In the spring of 1943, flying a P-40, Lieutenant DI Koval of the 45th IAP, managed to shoot down his fifth enemy aircraft, thus acquiring the status of "ace": fighting on the North Caucasus front, he destroyed a total of six German aircraft.
Several units equipped with the P-40 achieved good results in combat, even if the number of P-40 aces remained lower than , for example, the P-39, which was the Lend-Lease fighter supplied to the USSR in the greatest number.
Reports from Soviet Air Force pilots show that they appreciated the P-40, particularly for its long range, which exceeded that of most Russian fighters.
Overall, they continued to prefer the Bell P-39 Airacobra, but considered the P-40 to be significantly superior to the Hawker Hurricane.
Pilot NG Golodnikov recalled:

«The cockpit was large and high. At first, the fact that the edge of the fuselage was so low and that, therefore, the windows reached our waists was unpleasant. But the bulletproof glass and the armored seat were sturdy, and the visibility was good. The radio was also good: it was powerful and reliable, although only HF. The P-40 could engage in combat with all Messerschmitts under equal conditions, almost until the end of 1943. Considering all the characteristics of the P-40, at that time the Tomahawk was equal to the Bf-109F, while the Kittyhawk was slightly better. Its speed and ability to maneuver horizontally and vertically were good and fully competitive with those of enemy aircraft. Acceleration was a bit slow, but once you got used to the engine, it was fine. We considered the P-40 a capable fighter.»

The main complaint of the Soviet pilots was, in fact, the low rate of climb, to which were added some maintenance problems related to engine wear: generally the VVS pilots engaged in combat with the emergency combat power engaged, which brought the speed and acceleration performance closer to those of the German aircraft, but ended up burning out the engines within a few weeks.
Other logistical difficulties were related to the higher fuel quality and oil purity standards required by Allison engines compared to Soviet-made engines.

- A number of "burned" P-40s were re-engined with Soviet Klimov engines, but their performance was rather poor and they were relegated to the second line.

In total, 15 entire United States Army Air Force Fighter Groups (FGs), along with a few scattered squadrons and tactical reconnaissance units, flew the P-40 between 1941 and 1945.
Due to its overall inadequate performance, the P-40 was replaced as soon as possible by the Lockheed P-38 Lightning,

the North American P-51 Mustang and the Republic P-47 Thunderbolt.
However, between 1942 and 1943 the bulk of USAAF fighter operations rested on the P-40 and the equally inadequate P-39; in the Pacific, in particular, it was these two fighters, together with the carrier-based Grumman F4F Wildcat, that did the most to counter Japanese air forces.
The P-40 was the USAAF's primary fighter in the Pacific and Southwest Pacific theaters during 1941-42: however, in the first major battles, at Pearl Harbor and the Philippines, P-40 squadrons suffered heavy losses both on the ground, in attacks by Japanese fighter-bombers and bombers, and in the air, in combat with Nakajima Ki-43 and Mitsubishi A6M Zero fighters.
When Japan launched its surprise offensive against American naval forces in Hawaii on 7 December 1941, 107 P-40s and P-40Bs were in the Pacific, but only four of them managed to get airborne to counter the unexpected Japanese attack.
Over the next four days, the 20th and 34th Pursuit Squadrons' P-40 numbers dropped to just 22 aircraft.

- Over Pearl Harbor, however, a P-40 piloted by Lieutenant George Welch achieved the first American aerial victory of the conflict.

During the Dutch East Indies campaign, the 17th Pursuit Squadron, made up of USAAF pilots evacuated from the Philippines, claimed 49 Japanese aircraft shot down against only 17 P-40s lost.
In the Solomon Islands and New Guinea campaigns, as well as in the defense of Australia, improved pilot training and some new tactics allowed the USAAF to successfully exploit some of the P-40's strengths.
To address shortages of spare parts and problems replacing downed aircraft, the U.S. Fifth Air Force and the Royal

Australian Air Force created a P-40 management and replacement network in late July 1942, through which aircraft were periodically moved from the front to the rear for necessary overhauls and repairs.
The USAAF's 49th Fighter Group flew the P-40 from the beginning of the war.
This is the comparison between the Curtiss P-40 fighter and the P-38 Lightning that one of the unit's pilots, Robert DeHaven, achieved 10 victories flying the P-40, out of 14 total:

"Flying wisely, the P-40 was a very capable airplane. It could turn tighter than the P-38, a fact some pilots failed to realize when they transitioned between the two airplanes. The real problem was its limited range. As we pushed the Japanese back, P-40 pilots were gradually taken out of the war."

Between 1941 and 1945, the 8th, 15th, 18th, 24th, 49th, 343rd and 347th Pursuit Groups/Fighter Groups flew the P-40 in the Pacific Theater : most of them switched to the P-38 in 1943-44.
In 1945, the 71st Reconnaissance Group employed some P-40s as forward reconnaissance aircraft during ground operations in the Philippines until the delivery of new P-51s.
The 1st American Volunteer Group was integrated into the United States Army Air Force in 1942, joining the regular American forces as the 23rd Fighter Group.

- The unit continued to fly more modern versions of P-40s until the end of the war, achieving a favorable ratio of enemy aircraft shot down to aircraft lost.

Other U.S. units arriving in the China-Burma-India Theater after the AVG continued to perform well with the P-40, claiming a total of 973 kills, or 64.8 percent of the total U.S. aircraft destroyed in that area.
Aviation historian Carl Molesworth states that:

" *The P-40 simply dominated the skies over Burma and China. By 1942 it was able to gain air superiority over free China, northern Burma and the Assam Valley in India, and never lost it again.* "

In addition to the 23rd FG, the 3rd, 5th, 51st and 80th FG and the 10th TRS reconnaissance also operated the P-40 in the Burma-Indo-China theater.

Some of these (the 3rd and 5th FG of the Chinese American Composite Wing) were composed of Chinese as well as American pilots.

In addition to being a fighter, P-40 pilots in this area also successfully used them as fighter-bombers: the 80th Fighter Group, in particular , used its so-called B-40s, P-40s capable of carrying up to 1,000 lb (454 kg) of bombs, to strike Japanese-held bridges.

- The Curtiss P-40 was also used extensively in the Mediterranean theater by several USAAF units, including the 33rd, 57th, 58th, 79th, 324th and 325th Fighter Groups.

The 57th FG pilots were the first USAAF P-40 pilots to see action in the Mediterranean, beginning in July 1942.

Although the P-40 suffered heavy losses in the MTO (Mediterranean Theater of Operations), many P-40 units achieved favorable kill-loss ratios against Axis aircraft: for example, the 324th FG achieved a ratio of enemy aircraft shot down to its own aircraft lost of more than two to one.

- In total, 23 U.S. P-40 pilots achieved "ace" status in the Mediterranean, shooting down five or more enemy aircraft, mostly during the first half of 1943.

As in the Pacific, these successes resulted largely from the pilots' experience and the employment of effective tactics.
The 57th FG was the unit most directly involved in the so-called "Palm Sunday Massacre" of April 18, 1943.
Decryption of some “Ultra” signals by Allied intelligence had revealed a plan to move a large formation of German Junkers Ju 52 transports across the Mediterranean, under escort by German and Italian fighters.
Between 16:30 and 18:30, all the wings of the 57th FG intervened with intense efforts against the enemy transport aircraft: the convoy, composed of more than 100 aircraft, was intercepted and in the clash that followed the P-40s of the 57th destroyed 74 opponents, including 58 Ju 52s, 14 Messerschmitt Bf 109 light escort fighters and 2 Messerschmitt Bf 110 heavy escort fighters.
Between 20 and 40 Axis aircraft were seen landing at Cape Bon, Tunisia, to escape attack: Allied losses amounted to 6 aircraft, including 5 P-40s.
On 22 April, during Operation Flax, a similar formation of P-40s attacked a group of 14 Messerschmitt Me 323 "Gigant" six-engined transports, escorted by seven Bf 109s of II./JG 27.
All transport aircraft were destroyed, with the loss of three P-40s.
The 57th continued to fly the P-40 until early 1944: by that date, the group had been credited with at least 140 aerial victories.
In early 1943, 75 P-40Ls were loaded onto the U.S. aircraft carrier USS Ranger: on February 23, during Operation Torch: pilots of the 58th FG took off from the carrier for Cazas airfield, near Casablanca, Morocco, which had recently been captured from Vichy French forces.
These aircraft were used to re-equip the 33rd FG: the pilots of the 58th were reassigned.
The 325th FG, known by the nickname Checkertail Clan, also flew the P-40 in the Mediterranean theater.

The unit achieved at least 133 aerial victories between April and October 1943, of which 95 were Messerschmitt Bf 109s and 26 were Macchi MC202s, losing 17 P-40s in combat.
An anecdote involving the 325th FG indicates the risks a Bf 109 could face in attempting to outmaneuver the P-40 in close-quarters maneuver combat.
Historian Carol Cathcart writes:

«On July 30, 1943, 20 P-40s of the 317th Fighter Squadron and 16 of the 319th took off on an air patrol with the intention of rendezvous over Sardinia. As they turned to head south over the western part of the island, they were attacked near Sassari, 20 miles north of the rendezvous point. The attacking formation consisted of 25/30 Bf 109s and M.C. 202s and in the short, intense fight the 317th destroyed 21 enemy aircraft.»

A famous unit of African-American pilots, the 99th Fighter Squadron, better known as the Tuskegee Airmen or Redtails, flew the P-40 in the first eight months of its service in the Mediterranean theater.
On June 9, 1943, the Tuskegee Airmen became the first African-American fighter pilots to engage an enemy aircraft, over Pantelleria: a Focke-Wulf Fw 190 was damaged by Lieutenant Willie Ashley Jr.
On 2 July, the squadron achieved its first confirmed victory: an Fw 190 destroyed by Captain Charles Hall.
The 99th FS continued to achieve successes with the P-40 until it was re-equipped with the P-39 in February 1944.
The Kittyhawk was also the main fighter employed by the Royal Australian Air Force in the Second World War.
Two RAAF squadrons within the Desert Air Force operating in North Africa, No. 3 and No. 450 Squadrons were the first to receive the P-40.

Many Australians achieved considerable success aboard this aircraft: 18 pilots became aces and at least five, by shooting down 10 or more enemies, achieved "double ace" status: Clive Caldwell, Nicky Barr, John Waddy, Bob Whittle (with 11 kills each) and Bobby Gibbes (with 10 victories).
They fought in the North African, Middle Eastern and New Guinea theaters.
Nicky Barr, like many other Australian airmen, considered the P-40 a reliable machine:

"The Kittyhawk became a friend to me. It could get you out of trouble more often than not. It was a real workhorse."

As the war in North Africa reached its height, the war in the Pacific was in its early stages and RAAF units in Australia were severely strapped for fighter aircraft.
Spitfire production was taken up by the war in Europe; the P-38 was beginning to be tested, but was difficult to obtain, while the P-51 had not yet reached operational service in any theatre, and the inexperienced Australian aircraft industry was oriented towards large aircraft.
Originally intended for the US Far East Air Force in the Philippines, but diverted to Australia following increased Japanese naval activity, USAAF P-40s were the first suitable fighters to arrive in the RAAF ranks in significant numbers.

- In Australia, the P-40 received the designation A-29.

RAAF Kittyhawks played an important role in the South West Pacific theatre: during the early years of the Pacific War they fought both as pure fighters and as fighter-bombers, capable of withstanding considerable damage and carrying 1,000 lb (454 kg) of bombs.
For example, No. 75 and No. 76 Squadrons were crucial during the Battle of Milne Bay, New Guinea, countering Japanese

aircraft and providing effective close air support for Australian infantry, denying the Japanese their initial advantage.
The RAAF units which made the most extensive use of the Kittyhawk in the South West Pacific were Nos. 75, 76, 77, 78, 80, 82, 84 and 86 Squadrons, which operated especially in New Guinea and Borneo.
Towards the end of the conflict, RAAF fighter squadrons began to switch to the P-51D, but the Kittyhawk remained in service until the end of the war, for example in Borneo.

- In total the RAAF acquired 841 Kittyhawks, not counting those ordered for the RAF and flown by Australians in North Africa: of these, 163 were P-40Es, 42 P-40Ks, 90 P-40Ms and 553 P-40Ns.

In addition, the RAAF ordered 67 aircraft which were used by No. 120 (Netherlands East Indies) Squadron, a joint Australian-Dutch unit also operating in the South West Pacific.

- The P-40 was withdrawn from RAAF service in 1947.

Some units of the RNZAF, the Royal New Zealand Air Force, as well as several New Zealand pilots serving in other air forces, flew the Curtiss P-40 in North Africa: among these units, belonging to the Desert Air Force, was the 112 Squadron of ace Jerry Westenra.
In the Pacific theatre, 301 P-40s were transferred to the RNZAF under the Lend-Lease arrangements, although four of them were lost in transit.
These aircraft equipped 14, 15, 16, 17, 18, 19 and 20 Squadrons.

- Between 1942 and 1944, New Zealand Air Force P-40s enjoyed some success against the Japanese: their pilots scored 100 aerial victories while losing 20 aircraft.

Geoff Fisken, the Commonwealth ace with the highest number of victories in the Pacific, flew the P-40 with 15 Squadron, although half of his victories were achieved flying the Brewster Buffalo.

Most of the RNZAF P-40s' aerial victories were achieved against Japanese fighters, particularly the Mitsubis hi A6M, better known as the "Zero": however, bombers such as the Aichi D3A "Val" were also reported.
The only confirmed kill of a twin-engine aircraft, a Mitsubishi Ki-21 "Sally", was claimed by Fisken in July 1943.

- From late 1943 and well into 1944, New Zealand P-40s were used increasingly against ground targets, sometimes employing depth charges as high-explosive bombs: the last remaining front-line P-40s were replaced by the Vought F4U Corsair in 1944, and were relegated to advanced training duties.

In mid-May 1940, at Uplands Airfield, near Ottawa, Canada, a group of officers witnessed a round of comparative tests pitting the XP-40 against a Spitfire Mk I.
Wing Commander FV Beamish, an RAF officer, and Squadron Leader EA McNab, RCAF, immediately realised that the P-40 was not as good a fighter as the Spitfire, although it was not without some merits.
However, subsequently, especially during 1941-1942, the Spitfire would not be available in sufficient numbers to equip all Commonwealth air forces, and so, from 1941 onwards, several units of the Royal Canadian Air Force found themselves flying the P-40, both at home and overseas.

- In total, 11 Canadian squadrons flew the P-40.

Four of them were deployed overseas (No. 400, 403, 414 and 430 Squadrons) and seven remained at home (No. 14, 111, 118, 132, 133, 135 and 163 Squadrons).

Canadians, like other Commonwealth pilots, also fought with the RAF and other air forces as well as the RCAF, for example, in North Africa, the Mediterranean and South-East Asia.

No. 403 Squadron RCAF, a fighter unit based at Odilham, not far from London, operated the Tomahawk for some time before switching to the Spitfire.

Two close air support (Army Co-operation) squadrons, No. 400 and No. 414 Squadrons, trained on the Tomahawk before being re-equipped with the Mustang: of these, only No. 400 Squadron used its Tomahawks operationally, conducting a series of bombing and strafing raids over occupied France in late 1941.

In January 1943, No. 430 Squadron RCAF was formed at Hartford Bridge, England, and trained on Tomahawk Mk IIAs (by then essentially obsolete) and received the new Mustang Mk I before commencing operations.

As for the use on the American continent, in early 1945, some P-40N pilots of the Canadian No. 133 Squadron intercepted three Japanese bomb balloons in flight over British Columbia: the three unmanned balloons, armed with incendiary bombs linked to timed devices with the aim of starting fires on the American coasts, were easily destroyed.

The Flying Tigers

The Flying Tigers, translated from the English Flying Tigers, was the nickname given to the 1st American Volunteer Group, an air group sent by the United States of America to Nationalist China to assist it militarily in the war against Japan during the Second Sino-Japanese War of the 1940s.
The group was formed under the command of General Claire Chennault on an initiative personally desired by President Franklin Delano Roosevelt, classifying as civilian employees the flight and support personnel coming from the ranks of the United States Army Air Forces (USAAF), the US Navy and the US Marine Corps: to give formal coverage to the volunteer nature of the participants in the enterprise, it was an essential condition that they had officially resigned from their military service.

- The aircraft used were American-built, essentially Curtiss P-40s, and bore the insignia of Nationalist China.

Its ranks included many aces of future fame, such as Gregory "Pappy" Boyington, who later became the founder of the "Black Sheep" squadron.
Under the leadership of Captain Claire Lee Chennault, a group of 109 pilots and 150 mechanics, plus a group of administrative personnel, arrived in the spring of 1941.
At that time, it took very little to organize an air force.
They were initially in Rangoon, Burma, and assembly of the first 99 fighters began there on 28 November.
The First American Volunteer Group (AVG) had three squadrons with 18 aircraft each, each divided into flights of six.

However, flight activity began only on December 10, 1941, so it is false, as is sometimes reported, that these Americans were fighting the Japanese even before the official war.

A P-40 of the 1st American Volunteer Group (the famous Flying Tigers) with the distinctive "shark mouth" decoration painted on the nose.

Since No.112 Squadron RAF had become famous for painting the sharkmouth around the front air intake of their Tomahawks, the Americans wanted to do the same, after seeing it in a newspaper report: so, despite being "copycats", they are often still considered the real inventors of the sharkmouth.
The P-40's air intake was large and placed under the nose: the Italian Macchi MC 202D had the same type of application experimentally, without success.
The first battle began on December 20, 1941, when a force of twenty P-40s took to the air and clashed with previously unopposed Army Ki-21 bombers, who suddenly lost three or six of their own to a P-40 that had landed off-field.

On 23 December the Japanese retaliated by directly attacking a Rangoon with 60 Ki-21s, 27 Ki-30s and an escort of about 30 Ki-27s.
The Flying Tigers were said to have destroyed another 10 bombers and one fighter against four of the dozen P-40s and two pilots: three more fighters were claimed by the 15 Buffalos of No.67 Squadron RAF, which however lost five aircraft and as many pilots.
Note how the sources differ, some say the victories were 6 bombers and 4 fighters vs 2 P-40s, plus another 6 bombers for the Buffalos, but these seem less accurate overall.
It was the Christmas Battle that created the “myth”, when 13 P-40s and 14 Buffalos fought other Japanese aircraft, whose various units are also known, and which included 66 Ki-21s, 27 Ki-30s, 32 Ki-27s and 25 Ki-43s.
The P-40s claimed 24 aircraft against two of them, the Buffalos, who insisted on maneuverable combat, had 4 victories but as many aircraft and pilots lost, so much so that at that point Squadron 67, after two battles, was already finished.
In reality, the battle most likely resulted in no more than 10 Japanese casualties, but another 8 fell into the sea after the battle. It was even said that an American pilot had 5 victories that day, but AVG records give him a total of 4.83.
The battle, however, won the respect of the Japanese and the praise of Churchill, who compared the AVG's impetus to that of the British BoB pilots.
On December 28, 1941, however, Japanese bombers suffered a nasty shock when 10 of the inexhaustible Ki-21s surprised the Mingaladon airfield and destroyed many structures and aircraft.
On the 30th the Hell's Angels squadron left Rangoon to be relieved by the Panda Bears who brought 17 aircraft.
The squadron commander used them offensively with strafing actions on enemy airfields, since these were too strong to leave him the overall initiative.

The Japanese tried to do the same, but on January 4 23 Ki-27s suffered 7 losses against P-40s, but then two bomber formations arrived with escorts of 30 fighters.

- The Americans claimed 6 bombers and 4 fighters, but had 4 aircraft shot down along with one pilot.

On January 8, one of the P-40s strafing the airfields was shot down and the pilot taken prisoner.

After the Japanese dealt with the P-40s, they carried out mostly night attacks on the airfields and Mingaladon was destroyed, with the aircraft necessarily diverted to nearby rice fields.

From there they continued to operate and escort British Blenheims and strafe enemy airfields.

Another battle on 25 February 1942, when 9 P-40s claimed 24 aircraft, and on 26 February they claimed another 21, results considerably in excess of actual Japanese losses.

At one point Chiang Kai Shek wanted P-40s to fly in support of Chinese troops, but these actions were too dangerous and resulted in losses.

In the meantime, Rangoon fell on March 8, when the P-40Es also arrived: since Chennault managed to convince the head of the Chinese Nationalists that the AVG should mainly carry out air-to-air actions, the pilots, who at a certain point had become exasperated and started a sort of strike, were then put back in condition to fight the war more congenial to them and, in one of the last days, they shot down another 11 Japanese planes.

In all, in just 10 weeks, the AVG claimed some 291 victories and another 76 probables.

In February 30 P-40Es also appeared, but on 1 May 12 or 22 P-40s had to be destroyed because the Japanese advance, which the AVG often countered on the ground as well, endangered their airfield.

Loi-wing airfield was abandoned for Paoshan, which however was destroyed by another Japanese bombing, so the Americans

had to return to Kunming, where the above-mentioned aircraft under repair were destroyed at some point.
On May 12, 1942, the Americans flew a 400-mile mission and strafed an airfield near Hanoi, killing 16 aircraft on the ground for one loss of their own.
On June 12th there were another 9 victories, on the 13th there was a clash against 9 Ki-21s, 4 Ki-27s and 5 new Ki-45s, with 11 aircraft claimed shot down including one of the new Ki-45s, against two P-40s but with the pilots safe.
On July 9, also because of the tropical rains, all activity was suspended. As for the bombers, which Chennault would have liked to establish first with 18 Hudsons, then with other types, only for 4 days was it possible to get one's hands on and use 4 B-25Cs, in July 1942.
On 9 July the AVG was incorporated into the USAAF as the 23rd Fighter Group with its 74, 75 and 76 Squadrons.
11 P-43 Lancers were also delivered, but were not used as they were considered unreliable (and extremely similar to the Japanese Ki-44s).
On July 9, 1942 the last casualty, Red Shamblin, was hit during a ground attack.

- In all, during the 30 weeks of operations 297 aircraft were claimed, 153 probables, but there were also 78 aircraft and 13 pilots lost in action, another 9 killed in accidents and 3 captured.

Other sources speak of 268 aircraft claimed in the seven months of activity, plus probable ones.
Of the P-40s only 12 had been shot down in air combat, 8 by flak, 13 by air raids on airfields, 23 in crashes (mostly during the acclimatization period) and 22 on fire.
Among the AVG aces the best was Robert Neale with 15.55 victories, even if those in air combat were 13 (perhaps he had

also had ground attack actions), perhaps the most famous was Tex Hill with 11.25 victories, but in total the aces were 26.
This result seems extraordinary and it is, but not to the extent that the Americans wanted it to be.
Post-war findings, as usual, show differences, as the Japanese Army Air Force would have had a lot of trouble operating if it had suffered so many losses in such a short time. According to later research, however debatable and contested, the total number of aircraft shot down would have been around 115 with as many as 400 airmen killed.
However, even so, this is an exceptional result, especially in terms of the reduction-loss ratio.
Among the pilots was the future ace Boyington, who had two victories, or perhaps 6, including 4 on the ground.
In any case, it is worth analyzing the progress of the battles.
First of all, the P-40 was far superior, if it had been used well, as it was, to the Japanese fighters.
The Americans obviously said they were facing clouds of Zeros, but luckily for them, this did not happen: initially there were only or almost only Army Ki-27s, later supplemented by some Ki-43s and a few Ki-44s.

- The P-40 was capable of flying at 563 km/h and carrying four 12.7 mm guns, two in the nose and two in the wings, although it became rather unstable above 7,600 metres.

Chennault apparently knew the results of a Zero captured by the Chinese in November 1940 and so informed his men that maneuverable combat was practically impossible with such opponents, but that maximum use had to be made of speed and firepower.
The three squadrons, therefore, already had the right tips to avoid getting involved in a field for which they would not have had sufficient qualities.

One of the P-40s was destroyed during the embarkation, the others became part of the squadrons, which as mentioned, were 3: the 1st "Adam and Eve", the 2nd "Panda Bears" and the 3rd "Hells Angels".

During training the heat caused many problems for men and engines, and three pilots were killed, in addition to several aircraft disabled.

But where did the volunteers come from? The US was still officially neutral, so they were recruited through a recruitment drive by the civilian CAMCO, which visited military bases.

The pilots had a salary of $260 per month, which was already good, but they were promised $600-750 per month while the ground staff were promised $150-350.

- Not only that, but there was also a reward promised by the Chinese of $500 per downed plane.

The P-40s began their activity with an aircraft that on 10 December 1941 performed a reconnaissance mission over enemy fields.

The P-40s mainly defended Burma, then Burma, because this was the only supply route for the Chinese to the rest of the world, via the Burma Road.

The P-40 fighters were fast compared to the Japanese aircraft, and well armed.

- The Ki-21 and 30 bombers were capable, but not effective enough at surviving enemy fighters.
- The Ki-27s were almost 100 km/h slower.
- The Ki-43s were about 50 km/h slower, and both armed with only two 7.7 mm guns, making them unable to absorb American fire or easily shoot down their opponents.

The fact that many American pilots saved themselves by parachute, despite the loss of their aircraft, can be explained by

the protection and robustness of the aircraft, especially in relation to the weak armament of their adversaries.
At high altitude, however, the agility and performance of the Japanese fighters were dangerous and there would have been a need to disengage if attacked, with a rapid dive.
The P-40 was, therefore, at an advantage, except in climbing and agility, over the Japanese.
But there was often too much emphasis in air combat: once, around February 1942, the P-40s claimed 15 Ki-27s when only 2 were lost, for example.
The tendency of unprotected enemy aircraft to catch fire was another cause of their losses.
At low altitude the P-40 was even faster than a Spitfire Mk I and a Bf-109E, and was also very agile.
Only at altitude did it suffer excessively from a drop in power, as would be seen in Europe.

Curtiss XP-46

The Curtiss XP-46 was a single-seat, single-engine, low-wing monoplane fighter aircraft developed by the American aircraft manufacturer Curtiss-Wright Corporation in the late 1930s and early 1940s and remained at the prototype stage.

- Built to replace the recently introduced Curtiss P-40, it differed visually in that it had a different landing gear, still concealed within the wing, but with a wide track and with the power legs moving inwards, rather than outwards.

When the P-40 entered production, its designer, Donovan Berlin, was already thinking about its successor.

The P-40 was, in fact, already considered obsolete even before it entered service, and the reactions of the Second World War in the European theater of operations had highlighted the need for more power, more protection and more efficient armament.

- However, due to the performance achieved during flight tests, which was inferior to that achieved by the P-40D, which was then entering production, its development was abandoned.

In September 1939, the United States Army Air Corps (USAAC), the then air component of the United States Army, issued a specification for the supply of a new model of fighter aircraft, contacting Curtiss-Wright, which was already equipping its units with the Curtiss P-40, to create a preliminary design for a more efficient aircraft suitable for use in the European theater of World War II.

- The requirements were for a single-engine, low-wing monoplane, slightly smaller than the P-40, and equipped with wide-track retractable landing gear.

For the engine, the choice fell on the Allison V-1710-39, a liquid-cooled V12 capable of delivering a power output of 1,150 hp (858 kW).

The Army ordered two prototypes from Curtiss under CP 39-13 on September 29, 1939: the designation was XP-46 and the serials were 40-3053 and 40-3054.

The two prototypes, designated XP-46 and XP-46A, were delivered to the USAAC, and the first flight took place on 15 February 1941.

To save time and get something in the air as quickly as possible, the second prototype (40-3054) was delivered without armament or radio.

- The performance of this aircraft was, however, very disappointing, with a maximum speed reaching just 660 km/h at 3,718 metres (12,200 ft), while this speed was that expected for a fully equipped aircraft.

The first prototype, fully equipped, flew for the first time on 29 September 1941.

Not surprisingly, since the aircraft was even heavier than the second prototype, its performance was nothing short of disastrous, with a meager 571 km/h reached at 3,718 metres (12,200 ft). Since the aircraft's performance was inferior to that of the P-40 then in service, the P-46 therefore offered no significant improvement over the P-40, and the program was cancelled.

The planned armament included two 12.7 mm caliber machine guns, positioned on the nose of the aircraft and synchronized to fire through the propeller disk, plus the possibility of integrating eight more, four on each side, 7.62 mm caliber, into the wing thickness.

- The maximum planned speed for the fully equipped aircraft was 659 km/h at an altitude of 4,572 metres (15,000 ft).

Some speculations held that the design of the North American NA-73X, the prototype of the future North American P-51 Mustang, was based on the development work of the X-46.

One of the two prototypes, seen from the side, shows the position of the ventral air intake of the radiators.

This is based on the $56,000 purchase by North American Aviation (NAA) of aerodynamic test data for the P-40 and XP-46 models: however, although there are some similarities in the location of the oil coolers between the two models, by that time the North American design was already at an advanced stage.

The USAAC later requested the adoption of self-sealing fuel tanks and an additional 29 kg (65 lb) of armor, modifications which proved to adversely affect overall performance.
In 1940, before a single prototype had been built, the British Purchasing Commission placed an order for the P-46 as a replacement for the P-40, which, under British Air Ministry designation conventions, was designated the Kittyhawk.
However, in June 1940, while the prototypes were being built, the USAAC ordered the company to give priority to the development of an improved variant of the P-40 to be equipped with the same power unit as the XP-46, also in order to avoid disruptions to the production line caused by any change to a new airframe.

- As a result, the UK government's order for the P-46 was cancelled, and the designation Kittyhawk was assigned to the new variant of the P-40.

Nonetheless, the two prototypes, designated as XP-46A, were, once completed, delivered to the USAAC, the first of which was flown on 15 February 1941, and sent on a series of comparative flight tests where their performance proved to be inferior to that of the contemporary P-40Ds.
Consequently, and also because the P-46 design did not offer significant improvements over the P-40, the program was definitively cancelled.
NAA's engineering department used British research into the Meredith effect, the ability of ventral placement of a radiator to optimize the aircraft's overall thrust.

Curtiss P-60

The Curtiss P-60 was an American single-engine, single-seat, low-wing monoplane fighter aircraft of the 1940s, developed by the Curtiss-Wright company as a successor to their P-40.
It went through a long series of prototype versions, finally evolving into a design that bore little resemblance to the P-40.

- None of these versions, however, reached production.

After the rejection of the XP-46, Curtiss submitted its Model 88 as a proposal to the United States Army Air Corps.

XP-60B with Allison V-1710-1 engine.

The design called for an aircraft using the P-40D fuselage and tail with a low-drag NACA laminar flow wing, the Continental I-1430-3 inverted V-12 engine (then under development), and eight wing-mounted 0.50 in (12.7 mm) machine guns.
This proposal was accepted and on 1 October 1940 a contract was issued for two prototypes with the aircraft designated XP-53.

Within two months the Army Air Corps approached Curtiss for an aircraft with a laminar wing and the British Rolls Royce Merlin engine.

Curtiss suggested using the XP-53 design and converting the second prototype during construction: the contract was amended to accommodate this, with the aircraft, known to the company as the Model 90, being designated the XP-60.

A Packard-built V-1650-1, equivalent to the Merlin Mk XX, as used on the Curtis XP-40F, was to be used. The airframe design for the XP-60 was modified for the different engine, and the main landing gear was changed from the rearward-retracting P-40 design to a new inward-retracting version, as used on the XP-46, which allowed for a longer pitch and a smooth wing surface when the gear was retracted.

This aircraft first flew on 18 September 1941 with a British Merlin 28 engine: the XP-53 prototype was later converted into a static test airframe for the XP-60.

Considering delays in delivery of the Packard-built Merlin engines, which could occur due to its use in other fighter projects closer to delivery, the use of a turbocharged Allison V-1710-75 engine was considered in its place.

This was expected to give a speed of 634 km/h (394 mph) at 7,620 metres (25,000 ft): accordingly, on 31 October 1941, a contract was awarded for 1,950 P-60A fighters using the Allison engine with deliveries scheduled for September 1942.

Flight testing of the XP-60 prototype did not proceed smoothly. In addition to landing gear problems, the projected maximum speed was not achieved due to deficiencies in the surface finish of the laminar flow wing, relatively high radiator drag compared to the North American P-51 Mustang then flying, and lower-than-specified engine power output.

The Allison P-60A engine did not produce the required 1,500 hp and now that America was at war following the Japanese attack on Pearl Harbor, delivery of existing designs took precedence over the introduction of a new design.

XP-60D with Merlin 61 engine.

Work on the P-60A was discontinued after 20 December 1941, when the USAAF recommended that Curtiss concentrate on license production of Republic P-47 Thunderbolts.

The P-60 project was not, however, stopped, but a decision was made to build an experimental aircraft on the XP-60 but with different engines. The new order issued on 2 January 1942 specified an XP-60A (Model 95A) with the Allison V-1710-75 engine and a General Electric B-14 turbocharger, an XP-60B (Model 95B) with the Allison V-1710-75 engine and a Wright SU-504-1 turbocharger, and an XP-60C (Model 95C) with the Chrysler XIV-2220 36.4-liter, 2,500-hp, 16-cylinder V-16 engine.

While the XP-60 wing would be used, the fuselage was more rounded in cross-section.

In February 1942, P-60A production was canceled so that Curtiss could build another 1,400 P-40s and to keep its production lines busy until the P-60 was ready.

At the time, the availability of the Chrysler engine was being called into question, and after Curtiss noted (in April) that the fuselage would need modifications or that several hundred pounds of ballast would be needed in the tail of the existing airframe to balance the heavier engine, the decision was made in September to install a Pratt & Whitney R-2800 radial engine in the XP-60C. Meanwhile, Curtiss installed a Packard V-1650-3, equivalent of the Merlin 61, in the original XP-60 with a four-bladed propeller and the larger XP-60A vertical stabilizer; this aircraft was redesignated XP-60D.

The XP-60A first flew on November 1, 1942.

While official interest in the type was waning, as new designs emerged, the promise of improved performance from the use of the R-2800 engine resulted in a contract for 500 aircraft, officially designated P-60A-1, with the R-2800 and contra-rotating propellers.

However, with concerns that contra-rotating propellers would not be available in time (Pratt & Whitney had to modify the engine gearbox), in order to obtain data, the XP-60B was modified to take the turbocharged R-2800-10 engine driving a four-bladed propeller.

As a result of the other prototype variants, this modification was redesignated XP-60E (Model 95D).

On 27 January 1943, the XP-60C flew for the first time, powered by an R-2800-53 engine with contra-rotating propellers: the aircraft's flight characteristics were deemed generally satisfactory.

The first flight of the XP-60E with the four-bladed propeller was delayed until 26 May 1943 , after it was discovered that, due to its lighter weight, the engine installation had to be moved 25 cm (10 inches) forward compared to the XP-60C.

In April 1943, the U.S. Army Air Forces decided to conduct an evaluation of the various fighter aircraft then in development and use, with a view to eliminating the less desirable designs.

Given four days' notice, Curtiss was asked to enter the XP-60E; however, since the XP-60E was not available, the company hastily readied the XP-60C (then under repair) for evaluation at Patterson Field.

The XP-60C performed poorly due to flaking wing finish, preventing laminar flow, and an engine that produced less power, resulting in production being reduced from 500 aircraft to 20 YP-60As and then to just two aircraft.

On May 6, 1943, the XP-60D crashed during a dive demonstration.

In January 1944, the XP-60E flew to Eglin Field for official trials, where USAAF pilots found that it did not compare favorably with contemporary aircraft designs.

However, when Curtiss suggested abandoning future work on the P-60 series, the USAAF insisted that at least one of the two aircraft already in production be completed.

Versions

XP-53

Curtiss Model 88; derived from XP-46 had a laminar flow wing and Continental XIV-1430-3 engine. Contracted for 1 October 1940, cancelled in favor of XP-60 in November 1941.
Two built, one converted to XP-60, the other used as a static test airframe.

XP-60

Curtiss Model 90: Rolls-Royce Merlin engine, armament eight 12.7 mm calibre machine guns.
Only one example built, first flight 18 September 1941, later modified to XP-60D.

XP-60A

Curtiss Model 95A: Allison V-1710-75 engine with B-14 turbocharger, armed with six 12.7 mm MGs.
Only one example built.

P-60A

Planned production version of the XP-60: 1,900 aircraft ordered, but all cancelled.

YP-60A-1

Pre-production version of the P-60A-1 with single propeller.

Twenty-six aircraft ordered, but only two built: one rebuilt as the YP-60E.

P-60A-1

Planned production version of the XP-60C with Pratt & Whitney R-2800-18 engine and counter-propeller.
Armament: four 12.7 mm MG machine guns.
500 examples ordered, but cancelled before any construction.

XP-60B

Curtiss Model 95B: V-1710-75 engine with SU-504-2 turbocharger.
Armament: six 12.7 mm caliber MGs.
Only one built, modified to XP-60E.

XP-60C

Curtiss Model 95C: Designed for the Chrysler XIV-2220 engine, built with R-2800-53 and contra-rotating propeller.
Armament: six 12.7 mm caliber MGs.
Only one built.
Rebuilt as XP-60E; original XP-60E rebuilt as XP-60C.

XP-60D

Rebuilt XP-60 (Curtiss Model 90B): Packard V-1650-3 engine.
Crashed May 6, 1943 at Rome Air Depot when tail separated in flight.

XP-60E

Rebuilt XP-60B. Curtiss Model 95D: R-2800-10 engine.
Crashed in January 1944.
XP-60C reconfigured to XP-60E state.

YP-60E

YP-60A-1 modified with bubble canopy. First flight 15 July 194: cancelled 22 December 1944.

XP-60F

Planned modification of YP-60A-1 with different model of R-2800: cancelled before conversion.

Technical Features

Dimensions and Weights

- Length: 10.34 metres (33 ft 11 in)
- Wingspan: 12.60 metres (41 ft 4 in)
- Height: 3.28 metres (10 ft 9 in)
- Wing area: 25.5 m^2 (275 sq ft)
- Empty weight: 3,901 kg (8,600 lb)
- Gross vehicle weight: 5,368 kg (11,835 lb)

Diet

- Powerplant: 1 x Pratt & Whitney R-2800-53, 18-cylinder air-cooled radial piston engine, 2,000 hp (1,500 kW)
- Propellers: 6-blade counter-rotating constant speed propeller

Performance

- Maximum speed: 666 km/h (414 mph) at 6,200 metres (20,350 ft)
- Autonomy: 507 km (315 miles)
- Tangency: 11,000 meters (35,000 feet)
- Rate of climb: 19.8 m/s (3,890 ft/min)
- Wing loading: 191 kg/m^2 (39.2 lb/sq ft)
- Power/mass: 0.31 kW/kg (0.19 hp/lb)

Armament

- 4 x 12.7mm Browning M2 machine guns

www.ingramcontent.com/pod-product-compliance
Lightning Source LLC
LaVergne TN
LVHW010118170826
845678LV00012B/2472

* 9 7 8 2 3 7 2 9 7 5 2 9 2 *